I Learned It From You

I0424820

KEVIN DOUGLAS WRIGHT

Copyright © 2019 Kevin Douglas Wright

ISBN: 978-1080820085

Wright Motion Picture Studios
www.KevinDouglasWright.com

CONTENTS

INTRODUCTION

"Sometimes What Someone Teaches Can Have Deadly Consequences. Are you in danger?"

This book is based on the 2019 documentary I Learned It From You, which was *Officially Selected* by three film festivals.

Global Indian Film Festival (Mumbai, India)
Independent Talents International Film Festival (Bloomington, Indiana)
CKF International Film Festival (Swindon, England)

The film was produced, directed, and written by the author of this book, Kevin Douglas Wright.

In the film and this book, Kevin interviewed six randomly selected people who were born between 1946 and 1953. He asked each of the interviewees the same six questions:

1. When were you born?
2. Where did you grow up during your childhood years?
3. What color were your childhood friends?
4. What childhood games did you play?
5. What is your earliest memory of someone pointing out to you that there is a major difference between being a black person [a person of color] and being a white person?
6. How do you see the future?

As each interview unfolds and each question is answered by each interviewee, their real-life stories consistently reveal someone *teaching* something that has been responsible for destroying people, cities, states, and countries, in front of our eyes, for hundreds of years.

The overall result of these interviews is that it is unbelievable how different people from different walks of life describe virtually identical negative experiences and feelings when answering these six simple questions.

The ideas, practices, and memories of slavery, discrimination, prejudice, and racism have become a part of everyone's life worldwide. The six interviewees described the effects of these ideas, practices, and memories on them as...

"Careers ruined, hate, fear, lives and hopes smashed violently and broken into pieces, disparity, animosity, discouraging behavior, feeling downtrodden, degradation, hopelessness, craziness, madness, reactions of hatred and anger, an extreme focus on skin color, stolen land, back-breaking work with low or no pay, work and sexual harassment, riots, oppression, injustice, and rape."

The world we live in today is extremely fast-paced. We do not have a lot of time. It is not easy for most of us to quickly get a civil rights lesson and read all of the history about:

Racist America, Jim Crow laws, civil rights then and now, conspiracy of lies, skin color, dark skin, light skin, oppression, segregation by design, racist behavior, Black Americans, White Americans, and the word nigger [also known as the n-word].

This book provides a snapshot of deeply rooted issues from six real people who have experienced the practices of discrimination and racism all of their lives. These six interviewees were born during the 1940s and 1950s [in 2019 their ages ranged from 66 to 73 years of age]. Their lives have been informed and governed by these practices.

Why does this story need to be told? At some point in our lives we will eventually have to decide the best way to handle or respond to an important issue, incident, or event. We may not have the time to jump on the Internet and spend hours, days, or weeks in an attempt to get a deeper understanding of every angle of discrimination and racism. *I Learned It From You* is a memorable way of seeing the effects of something so deeply rooted.

Tomorrow or the next day, we all will interact with people who are not like ourselves—white, black, interracial, a person of color or someone who is Jewish, Hispanic, Latino, Asian, Native American, lesbian, gay, physically challenged, or mentally challenged. The *"labels"* we give each other are endless, but...

The question is: What will *'you'* teach them?

I Learned It From You is a gentle reminder that... sometimes what someone teaches can have deadly consequences. Are you in danger? What will someone teach you?

—Kevin Douglas Wright

CHAPTER 1 — YEAR OF BIRTH

"When Were You Born?"

The interviewer and filmmaker, Kevin Douglas Wright, introduced everyone to the audience by asking, "What's your name?".

The first interviewee replied, "My name is Maggie."

***

"My name is Steven," said the second interviewee.

***

The third interviewee responded with, "Hi, my name is Gloria."

***

"My name is Margie," added the fourth interviewee.

***

The fifth interviewee responded, "My name is Miriam."

***

The sixth and final interviewee ended with, "My name is Mike."

***

Kevin moved on and asked, "When were you born?"
  "Yeah, I was born in 1953," replied Maggie.

***

"1950," Steven confirmed.

***

"I was born in 1950," Gloria answered.

***

"1946," added Margie.
  "1946?" Kevin clarified.

***

"I was born in 1952," Miriam replied.

***

"I was born in December of 1951," said Mike.

Summary

The six interviewees were all born between 1946 and 1953. When the documentary was filmed in 2019, the interviewees ages ranged from 66 to 73 years of age.

CHAPTER 2 — BORN AND RAISED

"Where Did You Grow Up During Your Childhood Years?"

Maggie was born in Jamaica. Her voice still carries that slight Jamaican accent, one that only a true native of the area could possess.

***

Steven was born in Fall River, Massachusetts, and grew up in Omaha, Nebraska.

***

Gloria is a second-generation Broward County [Florida] resident, and her grandfather bought some land in the Deerfield Beach area in Florida.

***

Margie was born in Washington, D.C., and grew up in Philadelphia, on West Oak Lane. When she was 13 her family moved outside of the city, to a suburb called

Broomall, and spent the first few years living with her grandparents until she was 16, when she "escaped" to Miami Beach, Florida.

***

Miriam was from Joliet, Illinois, not far from the bustling city of Chicago.

***

For the first couple years of his life, Mike lived in Anderson, South Carolina. His mother soon left the area, bringing him to Fort Lauderdale to live with his aunt and uncle when he was around two or three years old.

This area was the first in Fort Lauderdale where the NAACP [National Association for the Advancement of Colored People] came in and started buying homes. His family was the last remaining white family in the neighborhood. One of his neighbors, he recalls, was a lawyer, the others were both school teachers.

"They were professionals, so they were not what you expect when you think of, or at least in those days, when you thought of black people, and that helped me to understand that people are people. That, plus the fact that I had a black nanny when I was growing up, that treated me better than my parents did."

Summary

The six randomly selected people were all born in different parts of the world and all eventually moved to Florida.

Maggie was a Jamaican-American born and raised in Jamaica. Steven was a Black American born in Massachusetts and raised in Nebraska. Gloria was a Black American born and raised in Florida.

Margie was a Jewish American born in D.C. [District of Columbia] and raised in Pennsylvania and later in Florida.

Miriam was a Black American born and raised in Illinois. Mike was a White American born in South Carolina and raised in Florida.

So far there is no sign in these interviews that someone is teaching something that had been responsible for destroying people, cities, states, and countries, in front of our eyes, for hundreds of years.

As the interviews continued, Kevin explored any possible clues from each interviewee's childhood friends.

CHAPTER 3 — COLOR OF CHILDHOOD FRIENDS

"What Color Were Your Childhood Friends?"

The people in the area where Maggie grew up in were predominately light-skinned; most of the kids she played with were of mixed race—"different shades"—as she says. One or two families of color moved to the area and were generally accepted by others in that section.

Many were in interracial marriages with mixed race children who all went to school together. Poor, rich, white dark, in between, all played together and went to school together. To a young Maggie living in Jamaica, color never seemed like an issue.

She grew up knowing her grandparents well. Her grandmother, with blue eyes and blond hair, was one of the sweetest people she ever knew, despite not having a lot of money.

"The whole area was like a mixing pot," Maggie recalls. "We never knew prejudice."

***

Steven moved to Nebraska around the age of eight or nine. "I grew up in the projects," he says. "Now, no one would think there are projects in Nebraska, but there were." He grew up poor, but he never felt poor.

Steven was aware there was something different about him and his family. It wasn't until high school or junior high school that he really became aware of how stark, how telling, and how influential that really was.

"It was always a sense that we were—we, meaning black folks—were a little bit different, had it a little bit harder. Not a little bit, a lot, and that was just par for the course," Steven says.

He went to a predominantly black grade school and junior high school, and then switched over to a predominantly white college preparatory high school.

"It wasn't all bad," he says. "The Jewish kids and the black kids at Omaha Central really got along, and really were tight, and hung out together, and I can remember just the sense of camaraderie between the two communities."

Steven lived on the lower east side of town, on 30th and Myrtle, while the Jewish community was on the west side, closer to 72nd street. These two communities bonded through a shared high school experience, despite their distance and their racial differences.

***

Gloria grew up on the west side of the train tracks in Broward County [Florida], with white Americans on the east side. She grew up knowing there were white children on one side, black children on the other, and they knew where they belonged. No one ever crossed their side of the tracks, because, in her words, Jim Crow was just that strict. White kids and black kids never played together.

Control—From 1877 through the 1950s, some white Americans used lynchings to terrorize and control black people.

"During the Jim Crow Era, everything was like them and us," Gloria says, about the relationship between white and black children in her area.

"It was not so much, for us, about the fact that they were here, or there, but, for us, I get the feeling that it was more a thing of how do I shelter my kids, and keep them from the ravages of Jim Crow?"

The Jim Crow Era—A time when white people and black people were always separated during activities such as...

...eating in a restaurant, drinking from a water fountain, using a public toilet, attending school, going to the movies, riding on a bus, or in the rental or purchase of a home, or in the rental of hotel rooms.

Jim Crow Laws—State and local laws that enforced the separation of white people and black people in daily life.

She pauses, then addresses how children grew up during the Jim Crow era.

"I was skeptical, fearful. I have no control over what happens to you when you're someplace else, and certainly I don't want you to be over there, in a white household, when something happens to you, no. Uh-uh, no way."

Death by Public Hangings—1877 through the 1950s— During these times, every black person knew that some white men could easily take them, torture them, hang them from a tree by their neck, and set them on fire in public in front of many white people who supported lynchings.

***

In Margie's elementary school, which was close to a Catholic elementary school, the majority of students were Jewish. Her neighborhood then had a mix of Jews, Catholics, and other Gentiles. At that time, there were no people of color in her neighborhood.

***

Miriam's neighborhood in general was pretty mixed. Her next door neighbors, to the right of her house, were white. She remembers seeing a little girl who lived there, but she doesn't say whether or not they ever played together. On the other side of the street was another white family, with chickens in the yard.

"Everybody had more than we did," she says.

***

Mike remembers his neighborhood ranging from all white kids, to a mix, to all black kids.

"Once the first family sold to the NAACP, their neighbors naturally had to sell, because they weren't going to be around black people. 'There goes the neighborhood,' one of these attitudes," he says, with a hint of mockery in his voice at the mindset of some of his white neighbors.

"Realistically, there's just as much racism on one side of this, as there is on the other, which I learned about down the road, once my children were grown."

Action Steps For Today

When you have a moment, think back to your childhood and reflect on the following questions.

1. What color were your childhood friends?
2. In general, is childhood a better experience if you grow up going to school and playing with many different types children?
3. Is our life experience better if we all learn the same things during our childhood years or does it really depend upon *exactly what practices we are taught*?
4. The following *extreme* practices were taught: *Control and Separation*. Did the <u>extreme practices</u> used to control black people, such as public hangings and burnings and the separation of white people and black people all contribute to deadly consequences and the destruction of people, cities, states, and countries?
5. Today, are you currently experiencing the effects of these <u>extreme practices</u> that were common and accepted between the 1800s through the 1950s (with variations of those <u>extreme practices</u> continuing today as you read this sentence)? What are you experiencing today?

You have a very busy schedule, but if time permits feel free to **Keep The Conversation Going** in **Chapter 7** by posting your answers, comments, and questions.

CHAPTER 4 — FUN AND HAPPINESS

"What childhood games did you play?"

When Maggie was a child, she played all sorts of ring games with other children. With an abundance of fruit trees in the area, she would just climb a tree on a hot summer day and pick mangoes to eat as a juicy snack.

The teachers at school would organize things for the students to do for fun, like plant propagation. She lived in a predominately farming area, so learning to grow was always part of the lesson plan. She always loved to garden.

"I'm so thankful that I was taught how to grow things. I think every child should have that opportunity. That was part of it, growing things, and, of course, harvesting, and enjoying it," she says.

Maggie was also part of the local Forage club, where they taught her basic survival skills, like animal husbandry —breeding and caring for farm animals.

Maggie enjoyed swimming and loved the ocean. Living in a coastal area, Maggie grew up close to the sea. As a Sunday treat, her father would load the family up in the car and drive down to the river, where everyone would sit together and fry fish while the children went swimming. Once in awhile, Maggie and the other children would even get a boat ride from some of the fishermen.

"It was beautiful, it was idyllic," she says, looking back fondly. "We didn't know anything about color, we didn't know anything about racism. It was nonexistent."

***

Steven's mother, as he says, was really enlightened, her mantra was "You're going to study! You're going to get good grades, you're going to apply yourself, you're going to do right, and you're going to represent the family right."

So, he hit the library, hit the books. He had friends with whom he hung out and partied, but only after he finished his homework, as per his mother's request.

***

Gloria played marbles, until she was 16 years old. (She blames marbles for why her knees are so bad nowadays.) Along with marbles, she, her friends and her siblings played hopscotch and jacks, if they were in the house. There was one cardinal rule in her father's house—you had to be inside before the street lights came on.

"Regardless of whether or not you got your point, or whatever, you're down on the ground shooting marbles and you know you got a chance to win but that street light, you know, across the street, [when that street light came on] you just darted in the house."

***

Once Margie was old enough to go out by herself, she

went ice skating and rollerskating, but most of her time was spent reading through the local library. She read everything they had in the kid's section, and by the time she was around eleven years old, she picked up *The Diary of Anne Frank*. She had to get the librarian to sign off on it, who said, "You've read everything here. Go for it."

Margie comes from a family of musicians, so she kept a little radio in her room and stayed indoors singing along to all the songs. Her mother even had a Steinway grand piano in her living room, and Margie would perform musical numbers while her mother played along. Once she learned to play, Margie would occasionally go down to the basement and play the old upright piano, left down there after the Steinway took over the living room.

As she got older, her interests became more focused on her friends and she spent time sneaking out at night to talk with them under the stars.

***

Miriam recalls a sad childhood without much fun, but she found magic in the small places. Her father would occasionally take her and her siblings to the old Sears store. Back then, a section of the store functioned as a tiny pet shop, and Miriam remembers walking in and seeing all the animals.

Once they came through the doors, there was a candy counter inside the store that sold Bon Bons and chocolate milk drops with cream in the center—her father's favorite. She remembers Snowballs, white golf ball-sized chocolates with a hazelnut in the middle, coated in sugar that sparkled like diamonds.

Miriam remembers standing, transfixed, looking up at this glorious candy counter.

"It was like magic to me," she says.

Throughout the years, she's never been able to find

anything quite as special as those original Snowballs.

"They were unmatched. So that was my happiness, I guess."

***

Mike's main interests as a kid involved the usual—kickball, marbles, hide and seek. Once he got out of school, he'd get together with groups of guys and girls to talk, laugh, and drink.

Action Steps For Today

When you have a chance, think back to your childhood and try to remember the childhood games you played. Think about the following questions.

1. Is it true that we all played some of the same types of childhood games as other kids no matter the color of our skin? Does this make all kids equal regardless of their race?
2. Why do things change when children get older? Exactly how does discrimination and racism enter into everyone's life?
3. Does someone begin to teach children something different as a they get older?

You have a very busy schedule, but if time permits feel free to **Keep The Conversation Going** in **Chapter 7** by posting your answers, comments, and questions.

CHAPTER 5 — BLACK AND WHITE

"What is your earliest memory of someone pointing out to you that there is a major difference between being a black person [a person of color] and being a white person?"

Before high school, Maggie never identified herself with any color. She was just a human being, having fun. Some people were light, some were dark—it didn't matter. There was love, there was respect, and racism was never on her mind. It wasn't until she got older, when she started studying the slave trade in her history class her first year of high school, that she started to see and hear things. She began to understand what was going on in the world around her, and started to question "why is it so?" It was history that opened her eyes.

Her grandmother and her father were both blonde with blue eyes. Her mother was mixed black and Indian with a little Chinese somewhere in the mix. Maggie grew up thinking she was white because so many people around her were white. When history class taught her the one-drop rule— that "to have one drop of black blood makes you black"—she realized and embraced the fact that yes, she was black; however, to Maggie, it didn't matter.

"Your parents could be white and black, mixed. You are still black. It doesn't matter, but I embrace that. The more of us the merrier."

Maggie and the other black women at her job liked to play with their hair, wearing wigs and hair pieces, and all sorts of things. One day, Maggie decided to wear an extra curly hairpiece—she thought it was pretty, and neat and clean.

During the morning meeting, the general manager of the company looked at her and said, "Who would want to spend time with her?"

Maggie felt anger boil up in her blood, but she had to keep it inside. She needed her job and she was good at it. But how dare he? she couldn't help but think.

Looking back now, Maggie wonders, "You know what? I wouldn't be surprised if he was one of those KKK guys. I would not be surprised."

None of the other employees in that meeting said a word to stand up for Maggie, except for a man from Sicily who said "No, you can't do that. That's not right."

The rest followed their boss like little sheep, or like ducks in a row. Not a whisper.

After this event, Maggie became sick, attributing her illness to the pressure of her job, believing that the stress was manifesting into physical symptoms. She developed more serious illnesses as a result and had to resign. As soon as she realized she could no longer work, she wanted to do something about that man who belittled her for how she chose to wear her hair. She wrote to the Equal Employment Opportunity Commission (EEOC) and explained in detail what transpired, not only regarding her own situation, but also concerning other people of color in the workplace.

She remembers another manager who worked at the company, a black woman also from Jamaica, who was immediately demoted when the new [white] General Manager walked in the office. He wanted his management staff to be all white, despite this woman being qualified, good at the job, and an overall nice person. Maggie received a letter back from the EEOC saying that this man was investigated, and subsequently, he was fired only two weeks after Maggie had left. They had gone into his office and gave him five minutes to pack his things and leave.

"That was sweet justice, as far as I'm concerned, but still, the hurt and the mental pain to some extent is worse than physical pain," Maggie says.

"If he had slapped me it would have cooled off, but to do something like that to someone, it stays with them through life. Not that it's going to diminish my belief in myself, but it is something that it makes me a little more cautious in dealing with others, and sometimes you might be wrong by shying away from a situation that might be perfectly good, but, because of that experience, it made me cautious."

There was still a disparity among darker skinned children, who did not have the advantage of receiving higher education. Between the cost of attendance, the cost of uniforms, and the transportation to these schools, most black kids' education had to end at high school.

After Maggie graduated high school, she applied to a bank in Kingston, Jamaica. She got the job, but saw there were very, very few darker skinned people. She was told later there was an advertisement in the newspaper for banking positions, but you had to be light-skinned. When Maggie applied, she had no clue that the ad existed. She was hired right away.

She remembers the interview process was easy, and she

felt like she was being looked upon as privileged because of her slightly lighter skin. This bothered her, because by then she had friends who were darker, and she couldn't understand why society had to discriminate against them like that.

"You have racism, even in our own race. That is something that is the most stupid notion that I've come across. If you're a little light skinned, and you're a little dark skinned, it goes both ways. There can be animosity, because of it. Stupid. Stupid."

***

Steven recalls one memory from the ninth grade that was burned in the back of his mind. His teacher, a white woman at a predominately black junior high school, asked his class a question.

"If boys join a fraternity, what do girls join?"

Steven had never heard of fraternity or sorority, so he answered, "Maternity." It seemed clever, and it was something he knew women did.

This teacher had found out that Steven had applied to a college preparatory high school, and stood him in front of the class after he gave his answer.

She told him, "you're too dumb to study with white kids. You need to think about staying right where you are, doing what you're doing." All of the other students just laughed.

This teacher eventually ended up as principal at an all-black high school. To this day, Steven wonders how many lives and hopes were dashed and how many careers were ruined by this woman. To prove her wrong, he went to a predominantly white high school and got As and Bs (while still goofing off from time to time), and received a scholarship—the result of a competition for scholarships at Columbia University, started by social worker Rodney Weed, and a white Jewish rabbi, Rubenstein, both of whom were Columbia University alumni.

Not only did Steven get the scholarship, but he also had the opportunity to go to any Ivy League school of his choice, as a result. The notion that somehow he wasn't smart enough, however, stayed with him. He learned that if he was going to be successful, he had apply himself and work twice as hard as the white boys to achieve the same level of success.

When he thinks back to when his teacher insulted him, his initial reaction was hatred and anger. To this day, he doesn't know why he didn't act out. The more emotional thing would have been to do something outrageous, run out of the classroom, or strike her, or curse her out—but none of that occurred to him.

He says of that day, "I went home, and I told my mother, and her response was very practical. She says, 'I don't give a damn what the teacher said. You're going to hit the books. Go study,' and I listened to my momma, and it worked out all right. But, you know how black mommas can be."

Steven's grandfather on one side of his family was full-blooded Blackfoot Sioux. The original immigrants, the colonists, stole land from the Sioux, from his grandfather and his father. His mother's side of the family was African. In other words, the colonists came over and took land from one side, then brought the rest of his family, on the other side, over to work that land as slaves.

Ten years ago, Steven was the head of an organization called the National Minority Supplier Development Council [NMSDC]. This organization was initially established to help minority businesses to do business with corporate America. There were 43 chapters all over the country when Steven started a decade ago.

NMSDC's goal was to essentially level the playing field so that black, Latino, Asian, and Native American people could successfully compete. The NMDC had partnerships with all the major car companies, and tech companies like Microsoft and AT&T. At that time, Toyota had just built a manufacturing facility in Austin, Texas. The president of Steven's local operation worked in Texas with Toyota to open up opportunities for minority businesses.

Later, Toyota opened a facility in Tupelo, Mississippi and Steven was asked to fly down. He said okay, but realized he had to drive to Little Rock, Arkansas first in order to catch the flight.

He called National Car Rental and told them, "I'm going to rent a car, because I've got to drive to Tupelo, Mississippi. I don't want any nonsense. I want a GPS system, and give me a Ford. Give me something, so I can get down there."

"Mr. Simms, we've got good news and bad news for you. The good news is we got you a car. The bad news..." they said, "is that the car is a red Hummer."

Steven pictured himself driving through the South in this candy apple red Hummer, making him an easy target for police, who might pull him over, but it was all they had left.

As he drove along, he called a friend and co-worker, a white man named Jim, who worked at the national headquarters. He wanted somebody to know where he was. Jim kept breaking up due to bad reception, and laughed when Steven told him about the car. To get Jim to take him seriously, Steven had to [jokingly] threaten him.

"Listen to me," Steven said, and Jim listened.

"Here's where I am. Here's the junction I'm at. I'm going five miles below the speed limit."

While Steven luckily didn't run into any problems on this trip, when he finally arrived, the woman who was head of the Austin chapter came up to him. She was Native American, but could pass for white.

"Look, we've got to leave tomorrow afternoon," she said to him. "Can I ride back with you to Little Rock?"

"No," Steven said.

"Look, I'll make it easy. I'll just lay down in the seat."

"No, hell no, because if the police spot me, and your head pops up, I'm gone. I'm gone." Steven wasn't laughing.

"Not only no, but stay away from my car. Don't go near that car."

"That's America," Steven says today. "If you don't think ahead, if you don't plan, if you don't process stuff, by accident, you get caught up in it."

The only Portuguese Steven remembers from childhood is the phrase "va para casa." Translation: Go home. He thinks back to hearing those words.

"I was four, five, six at the time, so clearly people wanted to get rid of me, even at a young age."

Steven remembers an amusement park in Omaha called Peony Park, not far from the downtown area. Up until the time Steven left Nebraska, black people weren't allowed to visit it. While working at the NMSDC, Steven had to go give a speech in Omaha, where the organization had a chapter. Of all places, Steven was to give his speech at Peony Park, giving him the opportunity to finally enter the park and talk about Omaha, Nebraska getting ready to do right by its minorities.

"It was kind of rewarding to close that loop," he says.

When Steven was around sixteen or seventeen, the Governor of Alabama, George Wallace, came to Omaha for his presidential campaign. Wallace hosted a rally at the Convention Center, and Steven joined many other young black, white, and Hispanic folks in protesting. Until a riot started.

An older white man walked by Steven and said to him, "Nigger, you ain't even supposed to be in here."

He remembers it distinctly.

"After being called that so many times, you get situational about it. Your perspective expands, or grows, or develops, and, like I said, I can either kick his ass, or just let him go about doing what he was going to do, and I was more concerned, me and my buddy, about observing, and having a sense, recording this in our minds, of what was happening. When the rioting started, I walked over, stood close to him, and he put his hands up, said, 'please, don't hit me,' and, to me, that was kind of a victory."

Around the same time, in 1968, Bobby Kennedy was also running for President. He came to Omaha, before his assassination in Los Angeles. Steven recalls being unable to find his sister and her friends, and when he finally located them, they were sitting around with Bobby Kennedy, talking politics in his hotel room.

"I can't imagine how valuable the experience was for her, and she took his assassination, death very, very hard, because she had just had this experience, of seeing, and talking to him, and communicating with him, and getting to know him on a personal level, but that was one of those times that you live, that something unique and special happens to you. Stays with you for the rest of your life."

Steven only had one run-in with the police when he was younger, as a driver. His mother owned a station wagon and he would often drive his friends around town. They were goofing off one day, when the police pulled them over. In that moment, Steven felt real, genuine fear.

"I had fear for myself, I had fear for the other passengers. I had fear that they were going to do some stupid stuff which would get me killed," he says.

"I remember saying a prayer to myself as the police officer got out of his car, walked up to his window. 'Lord, get me out of this, and this will never happen again'."

Steven could tell immediately this was a white officer. He asked what they were up to, that somebody had complained about young people yelling out the windows of a car.

"Officer, I don't know anything about that," Steven said, and managed to catch some good luck.

"Okay. Well, where are you headed?" the officer asked.

"I'm just taking my guys home, and then I'm going home."

"Okay, well, let's see you do that."

So Steven dropped his friends off and went home. He doesn't remember if he ever let them in his car again, but he knows they weren't doing whatever the police had said, making noise, or being loud. But from then on, he walked the "straight and narrow".

"Lord have mercy!" Steven laughs about the incident today. "It's funny now. But it wasn't funny then."

Gloria's earliest memory of being at war with prejudice dates to grade school, when she and the other kids questioned why the books they were getting were already written on or had the pages torn out. They wanted to know why they couldn't have books like the other kids—new, clean books. The front covers of these books had a ledger where everyone who had owned the book before could write their name. Gloria remembers seeing ten names in one book; she recalls seeing the names but not knowing who they even were.

Around 1955, Gloria's father bought a car and took the family on a trip to Georgia to see his mother and relatives. Gloria never understood why they couldn't stop somewhere to eat. They had to pack and prepare everything they needed for the entire trip. If they had to relieve themselves, they had to stop along the road and go in the woods. They wouldn't dare try to stop at a gas station, or filling stations as they were called then, let alone sit down and eat somewhere. Even the car had to be in immaculate condition so it wouldn't break down along the way. Gloria always wondered why.

When she was growing up, during segregation, the Historically Black Colleges and Universities (HBCUs) would visit various black schools to give presentations. Gloria attended one of these presentations where she met a lady named Mary, who she will never forget. Mary came to give a presentation for Bennet College when she was in eleventh grade, and at that moment Gloria said "that's where I want to go to school." And she did.

When Gloria looked in the Bennet College yearbook she saw people of color, but they were lighter than her. The comparison between her complexion and theirs didn't mean much to her until she came back to her hometown and ran into one of her old teachers—who was very fair-skinned as Gloria recalls, but who was still considered black American.

"Gloria, I understand you did well for yourself," the teacher said to her.

"Yes…it depends upon what you call well," she said.

"Well I heard you got into Bennet College and then you pledged AKA [sorority]. And look at your skin color!"

Gloria looks back on this interaction with anger.

"Do you know how that made me feel? Out of all that I'd done, here's one of my teachers telling me this. What did you expect of me? I have no doubt that some of us, and, of course, have proved it here in later years, that there is discrimination between lighter skin and darker skin."

There was a drive-in theater in the town Gloria lived in. Black people couldn't go to it—there weren't any signs, but everyone just knew it and nobody challenged it. To get around it, however, Gloria and other black kids would sit on the cars or in the yard and watch the screens. While they could never hear the sound, they could see the same movies white people saw and for them, that was okay.

Gloria and a lot of people her age in the South just did what they had to do. They knew the boundaries.

"I always like to think, and I tell people all the time, I could never have been a slave, because I probably would have been a rebellious slave, because you start questioning. Kids question, as to why? Well, mommy, why can't we go over there and hear the sound, whatever? Hush girl, you know? That's just the way it is, and so we lived with that."

At 26 years old, Gloria returned home to Florida. She had no doubt that the jobs she had previously applied for had been given to other people, simply because they were white Americans. When Gloria came back, she had a Master's degree and work experience under her belt, but somebody else got the job, with no greater qualifications.

To this day, Gloria only regrets all the people who have come to Broward County, Florida from wherever (or whatever country) they may be from who don't know what Gloria and other black Americans went through during the Jim Crow era, and still look at them as second-class citizens without knowing the history of oppression.

Gloria used to play outside with friends who were lighter in complexion than her, and her mother used to call her inside saying, "Girl, come in the house, because you're going to get dark."

And she would always tell Gloria to never drink coffee, or it would make her darker. She wasn't allowed to wear colors, always navy blue or black, because she was a "colored kid." She couldn't stand out. Today, though, Gloria drinks a cup of coffee each morning and her favorite colors are bold pinks and greens.

Gloria reflects on her dark skin.

"You go and read some of the books, and they'll tell you the lighter ones among us, if we could do that, because things were so bad during Jim Crow, in the South, or whatever, because you have to understand that you're still coming off of slavery here, where the master has raped somebody—because I doubt a lot of those things were consensual—and they have these light skinned children. If they were light enough to pass, if you go back and read up on it, it would tell you that they went northeast, severed all ties, and they prayed that if they had children they wouldn't come out looking dark as me, or you [the interviewer]."

Gloria's father walked with his brother all the way from Georgia to Florida. They had no transportation and slept in the woods because they knew they couldn't be out in public on a journey like this. They didn't know anybody along the way where they could seek safe harbor, but sometimes they met some well-meaning people who were more welcoming. Somebody who might slip you a soda, or a meal, and then you'd go on your merry way. People who saw everyone as family.

A lot of times, though, people on these journeys would get caught up with the wrong white person and they would never make it to where they were going.

To Gloria, it was, and still is today, all about a person's sense of entitlement.

"You aren't entitled to anything, other than the breath that you breathe, that God gives you, and it does not say to me that you ought to be going around treating people any kind of way, or just like they don't matter on this earth, because we certainly do."

***

When Margie moved to the suburbs as a child, she heard her mother remark that "If the neighbors don't stop I'm going to sell the house to some Negro."

Margie says of her mother, "She never was overtly racist. I think she was just a nasty person. I don't think she was really hating black people. She was just as nasty to me."

When Margie was seventeen and living in Miami Beach, her grandfather became ill. She used to take the bus over to Mount Sinai Hospital to go visit him every day. The bus driver was a young black man from Miami named Nick.

After her grandfather's death, Margie went on the bus again to look for Nick, just to sit there, listen, and talk to him. Eventually Margie and Nick started dating. This was when the differences between black people and white people in the South became apparent to her.

Nick would pick Margie up at a bus stop, close to her house on the Venetian Causeway—but instead of getting in the front seat, Margie would sit on the floorboard of the car. Margie and Nick started dating in 1963, when a black man seen with a white woman would be in trouble. From there, the two would drive over to Sir [Saint] John's, the only integrated bar in Miami Beach—aside from the gay bar, Bell Bart's, where lesbian women took Margie under their wing—and they would end the night at Saint John's Hotel. This hotel's bar was always very dark, which appealed to the mixed couples in town who often partied there together. This, to Margie, was the only place that her and Nick never had to worry about being seen together.

At this time, Margie's uncle was a DJ at one of these clubs. When he'd come home to visit, he'd always bring with him a little tape recorder. He'd go around hotels in Tennessee, making appointments with singers and musicians like Bud Sopel, Johnny Mathis, and Ella Fitzgerald to have them record in his hotel room.

One of those days, he came back upset, agitated, throwing things around the house. One of the artists he was to record with was a black woman, who wasn't allowed to stay in the Fontainebleau, the very hotel that she was set to perform at later that evening. Instead, she had to stay across the street at a tiny motel. This deeply upset Margie's uncle, who was only trying to record talented singers and musicians, regardless of color.

It wasn't until Frank Sinatra came to Miami Beach for a show and called one of those hotels to say "I'm coming down with Sammy Davis, and if we don't walk in the front door, and stay here, you'll never see us again," and it worked. Sinatra, in his own way, was one of the first to work towards integrating the hotels in Miami Beach. There was still a ways to go, however, since any person of color who worked in the area had to be out of Miami Beach by sundown or they would be arrested, chased out of town, or worse.

Margie only has three or four memories of her life before the age of five and most of them involving a woman named Gay Phillips, who worked as a nanny for Margie's mother and grandmother. Gay was always sweet and kind to Margie, who would run home at lunch time on Fridays just to sit and talk with Gay while she did the ironing in the basement. When Margie was ten, her mother fired Gay.

Margie still refuses to believe the nasty things her mother would say about Gay Phillips. The lightbulb moment came when her mother lost a few pieces of jewelry, first blaming it on Margie, but then using it to accuse Gay of stealing so she could fire her. At a young age, Margie recognized the racism perpetuated by her mother, and has continued through her life to judge people by their heart, not their skin color.

***

"I must have been in kindergarten," Miriam says, remembering the moment when she learned the perceived differences between white and black people, "and we all went to this school called Park School that we walked to, and that was back in the days when they let kids my age walk. It ain't like that now, but we'd walk back and forth to school."

"I was five years old, walking by myself back and forth to school. I was passing this apartment building on the corner of Ohio Street on the way home, and there were these dirty little white kids playing in the yard, and they were filthy. Just nasty looking, and they was calling me, 'nigger! nigger!' and I looked at them. I was like, 'I don't know what that is, but it definitely doesn't sound good,' and so I was like 'I better find out what this is.'"

"So that's when I first came home, told my mother. I said, 'Ma, what is a nigger?' That's when I got my first civil rights lesson, and it was very discouraging."

*The N-Word: the word used to insult a black person who has
been systemically subjected to discrimination and unfair
treatment. It is one of the most offensive racial slurs.*

Miriam remembers feeling downtrodden after this conversation with her mother. The feeling of hopelessness.

Later in her life, in 1975, Miriam became a part of Cleveland history, when she became Cleveland, Ohio's first female sheet metal apprentice. She went to work as an apprentice in Brooklyn, a suburb of Cleveland, where, for the first time, she experienced real issues related to her race and her gender. The men would watch her while she worked, like tourists peering at animals in the zoo. She felt like a monkey in a glass cage. Most of the men she worked with were white, as there were very few other black people with the job.

Miriam was sexually harassed at work by men who thought they owned her as a woman, and a woman of color at that. Soon, she found them following her into the bathroom, watching her while she was behind the stall. Once, a married white man asked her to find a girl friend so that he and she could go on a double date together. Miriam sadly remembers multiple inappropriate incidents that happened to her during this time.

The harassment ended, for the most part, when Miriam was sent out to a job site when she was twenty-two. Someone handed her an enormous elbow of duct pipe, weighing fifty pounds at least, and sent her up a ladder. It wasn't safe at all, and Miriam didn't know if they were setting her up to discourage her or to drive her away, but she did it anyway and made it up to the top.

"Now, you have to attach it to that pipe and hammer it in," one of the guys called up to her.

She'd have to be strong enough to stand on the ladder,

hold the fifty-pound pipe with one hand, and hammer it in place with the other hand. It all truly showed her the dangers of being a sheet metal apprentice, but it never kept her from changing black history in Cleveland.

***

Mike remembers the Woolworth's store back in the mid to late '50s, which had two water fountains right next to each other—one white, one colored. When his cousin was using the one water fountain for white people, Mike would just go to the other one.

He didn't see the difference until someone said to him, "You can't drink from that one. It says right on there, colored."

Mike didn't even know what colored meant at that point. He had no idea of the oppression behind the word 'colored'.

In the late '50s, early '60s, when Mike was in junior high, when riots broke out in his school, he really began to see that everyone around him thought there was a notable difference between black and white. Mike, being one of only two or three white kids at the school, climbed a ladder that led to the top of the gymnasium, where he would sit and observe the police raid the school and watch the insanity breaking out among the hallways. Once everything calmed down, he'd climb back down and go home, taking the side streets to make sure he was actually safe. He wanted to stay out of people's way, like he was when he was on top of the gymnasium or somewhere hidden where people couldn't easily put their hands on him. He saw it as self-preservation.

Over the years, Mike developed a thicker skin towards people who had racially-biased attitudes. When he was eleven, his mother met a man who would later become his stepfather. By the time Mike was thirteen, his stepfather joined the Ku Klux Klan [KKK], because it opened avenues for his career as a businessman.

Loans, government contracts, and official business documents were all given to him merely because he was a Klan man. Mike was old enough to understand this was not a good thing.

Before his stepfather, Mike had never given any consideration to the Klan. Even growing up around black people, Mike recalls that it wasn't something they spoke about. He later discovered the amount of fear and anxiety behind the KKK, and he understood why his peers stayed silent.

Mike's stepfather hated it when he would talk about the black guys on his football team. Mike thought it was just so cool to have friends that were different than him. He brought one of his friends over one weekend, a kid named Paul whose parents had gone out of town. Mike thought it would be fun if Paul came over to his place and had dinner with him, so he wouldn't be alone.

When his stepfather came around the corner towards the kitchen table to see a ninth grader almost as big as himself, sitting and having dinner, talking back and forth with Mike, he was fuming. He turned right back around and sat down in his chair in the living room, put his feet up, ate the dinner Mike's mother brought him, and kept his mouth shut until Paul left. Then he approached Mike.

"Don't you ever do that to me again," he said.

"What? What'd I do to you?" Mike said, confused. As far as he was concerned, he'd stayed out of his way and hadn't bothered him.

"That doesn't happen here."

Mike then realized his stepfather was talking about Paul.

"He's a friend of mine. His parents are out of town, and his grandma doesn't get out of work until late. He came over for dinner, we were just eating."

"Not in my house," he snapped. "He's not really your friend. You don't even know him."

Mike stayed locked in his room almost the whole time he was growing up, right up until the day he moved out.

His stepfather's views never changed. For the rest of his life, he was just as hateful and racist.

Mike, however, continued to learn more about race and racial tensions down the road, even after starting his own family. When his son was in the first grade, attending Martin Luther King Elementary School, he got into the McKnight Achievers, a black organization that promoted education. If a student was doing well in school, they had the opportunity to join and have teachers mentor them, give them extra credits, and help them with their schoolwork.

Mike's son was the first white kid who was recommended to the McKnight Achievers, so Mike and his wife attended the membership ceremony. He remembers seeing all the black families and this one little white boy. Then the mumbling started, and the whispering, but nobody said anything derogatory to Mike, his wife, or his son. They sat through the ceremony, having a good time as they watched their son receive his jacket, a symbol of membership in the club.

As they were leaving, someone put their hand on Mike's shoulder, saying "You shouldn't come back."

Mike just looked at him. "That's okay," he said, and kept walking.

Later, Mike's wife, scared of the racialized tension, said to him, "I'd rather he didn't go," and he never went back to the club, despite qualifying for it as a good student.

Mike realized at that moment that racial tensions run both ways. "The difference being," he says, "that I can understand why the black people get so upset with the white people. I don't understand why white people get so upset with black people. I can understand why, in the black families and the black neighborhoods, they feel the way they do. The oppression, the anger, the injustice, the bull. That's driven these people. I'd have been nuts. I would have actually been nuts. I don't know if I could, personally, take that, and still say yes sir, no sir to anyone."

Action Steps For This Weekend

Over the weekend, think about the first time in your life that someone made it very clear to you that there is a major difference between *being a black person* and *being a white person*. Then, reflect on whether or not the following questions have answers?

1. Why would one group of people go through such great efforts to systematically control, separate, terrorize, and oppress another group of people?
2. Does **forbidden knowledge** exist? What is it anyway? Is there really true information out there that is being silenced?
3. Does everyone have a profound educational moment about racism that contributes to the direction of humanity? The very moment that the *black vs. white difference* is introduced to someone, doesn't that moment become one of *teacher and student*. Isn't racism simply a **learned behavior**? Someone *teaches* racism and a *student* learns racism.

4. Is there a conspiracy of lies where the goal is to keep groups of people in conflict with each other? Or, is this simply a case where the "people in power" do not want to spend time and money trying to convince everyone that **the real reason why** they do not like someone's skin color is *simply because they were <u>taught</u> not to like someone because of their skin color?*

5. In this chapter, was it easy to see that in the past... someone taught someone how to behave, someone learned that behavior, then used that behavior against someone else, and everyone together played a part in *"destroying people, cities, states, and countries, in front of our eyes, for hundreds of years"*? For what reason? What was the benefit? Why?

This Sunday, kick back and relax. If you find yourself with some free time, please take a moment to **Keep The Conversation Going** in **Chapter 7** by posting your answers, comments, and questions.

CHAPTER 6 — THE FUTURE

"The future? Do you see it getting better? Do you see that something still needs to be done?"

When asked if she sees the future improving, Maggie responds, "There is a feeling to me that our race is in danger, and unless we do something to protect it, it's going to get worse. We have been hurt from so many angles, and this is one human being against another human being. It shouldn't be so. There should be laws protecting, whether you're pink, white, purple, black, blue, that something like this should never happen again."

She recognizes that we can't change the past, since it's gone and we have no control over that, but she thinks we can learn from it and make sure it doesn't happen again.

"Look at what happened in Germany, under Hitler," says Maggie.

"They were intelligent, educated people, who saw what was going on, but I don't know, they got caught up in this thing, and, before you know it, Jews were being... Oh my gosh! What they went through. Not only Jews, blacks also, were being wiped out. Look at the horrors of their experience. The same thing can happen again, if we are not proactive. It can happen again. Let us learn from history."

Maggie wants to emphasize that she believes that not all white people are racist. She knows from her own experience that actions speak louder than color. She's taken Martin Luther King's dream to heart, repeating his words when looking towards the future.

"The color of a man's skin should not dictate how he's treated. The content of his character is what should be taken into consideration," she says.

***

When Steven thinks about surviving the Middle Passage, surviving slavery and Jim Crow—which to him was just another form of slavery—it reminds him of the strength and tenacity of his community in pushing forward.

1877 through the 1950s —During these times, many of the people guilty of kidnapping, torturing, hanging, and burning black people were never, ever punished for their crimes.

When Steven thinks about how the Supreme Court ruled his people [black people] as three-fifths of a man, less than human, it shows the kind of degradation they've continuously been subjected to.

"To have survived that, with our dignity, our passion, our empathy, and [our] compassion still intact, there's nothing we can't do. There's nothing we cannot accomplish if we put our minds to it."

Steven wishes he could somehow express to young black children today just how powerful they are, how they are the opposite of the stereotypes placed upon them. He thinks young people have to help out just as much as his own generation, and he would love to see more of these kids absorbing and believing the message that they too can accomplish whatever they set out to do.

To this day, he still worries when he walks out of his house and goes out into his neighborhood because where he lives in Florida, they still have a "stand-your-ground" law. It wouldn't surprise him, as a larger black man in the South, if someone shot him on the street and then said something along the lines of "Look at him, I thought he was attacking me." He knows that black people still have to be careful living in the United States.

"We have to think, and we have to impart that to our kids. At the same time, support them, and empower them, and have them understand how miraculous and divine they really are," he says.

"What each of us survived, each of us contributed to the stew we call America, and at some point America's got to decide to live up to its ideals, and it will be the better country for doing it, but, as Churchill said, 'America will always do the right thing, after it tries everything else,' so racism still exists post Obama."

Steven thinks America is the planet's great hope; he emphasizes again that there's nothing we can't do when we set our minds to it. It gives him hope seeing young people with friends who are Hispanic, or Asian, lesbian or gay, physically or mentally challenged who are still being able to say, "Yeah that's my buddy. That's who I run with." He thinks that once the older generation, which still holds onto the hate-filled attitudes of the past, passes on, new seedlings will take hold and grow, and America can continue to move forward.

"I'd like to think America has been the greatest

experience, experiment that this planet has ever seen," says Steven.

"Right now, we're going through a period where we're being tested, and whether we can stand up, retain our values, retain our sense of self, and do the right thing for the right reason. We'll see how this turns out."

***

Gloria's grandfather was always a stickler for education. He made no bones about it. His favorite saying was, "Once you get it up here in your head, nobody can take it away from you." If nothing else, he made sure Gloria got that education.

"That's a little bit about what we did, and how we did it back then," Gloria says. "It was them setting the stage for us, and letting us know that 'I want more for you than I had, or [more] than your mother had,' and each generation has built on that, one way or the other."

When Gloria came back from Howard University, she got a job in Miami, at Florida International University—around the same time when schools were still discriminating against people of color. Her job was to run a program that brought parents and students from different racial backgrounds together to try to help them to understand each other's cultures. During that time, Gloria found that once you're ignorant about somebody else's life, or the situation they're in, that is when you have the most prejudice—and she still finds this true today.

"When you understand about another person's life, or their culture, or whatever the case may be, then you're more likely to be not a racist basically, so what we would do, we would take these mixed families to restaurants together. We would have them go into each other's homes, and we got a grant from the government to do that," Gloria says.

Gloria wanted to bring the same type of program to Broward County. She wanted Broward citizens to get to know each other so they could do away with some of the racism and the name calling. One day in Fort Lauderdale, Gloria ran into the director of the Urban League.

"What are you doing nowadays?" he asked her.

"Oh, I'm still down in Miami," said Gloria.

"Look," he said. "They have a job offer for a Director of Human Rights in Broward County, and you need to be that next director. Where's your résumé?"

Gloria, who always carried her résumé with her, handed it to him, and the two went their separate ways. Lo and behold, a few days later, Gloria got the call and agreed to interview for the job.

"I said 'I already have a job,' but thinking at the back of my mind 'there's more money, and look at all the good you could do,' … I went in, and I paneled for the job. Obviously, I did very well on it, but here was the clincher."

At the interview, Gloria met an older Jewish woman named Kay who was also paneling for the job. Kay was currently working as the Assistant Director, but was interested in the higher position. The two spoke at length and got to know each other while waiting for each of their interviews. A few days later, Gloria got a phone call, offering her the Director position. Shocked and elated, she graciously accepted.

Gloria soon became good friends with both Kay and her husband, both of whom passed for white. They were originally from Monroeville, Pennsylvania, and would later move back.

"Gloria, I'm so glad you're here," Kay said to her while they were having lunch one day. "[Did you know] they wanted me to take that job, and after meeting you and seeing your credentials, I said to them, 'this is not a job for me. You have a very competent young black female, who can do this job, and you need to offer her the position.'"

When recalling this moment, Gloria tears up—not out of sadness, but out of gratitude. Kay could have just as easily taken the position for herself, insisted it go to Gloria, who Kay knew was more deserving. Gloria says she will never forget that lunch, or what Kay did for her in requesting Gloria for the Director of Human Rights position.

Kay worked as Gloria's Assistant Director until the day she retired. Between what Kay brought to the table and what Gloria contributed, the two women had a great time working together. They filed charges against people for discriminating against African Americans in housing and employment situations.

"With God's sense of humor—and I always look at it like this," Gloria says, "I tell a lot of people this. He has a way of making us get together, regardless of whether or not we want to. That's why you see so many interracial marriages, or whatever the case may be. All this stuff is going to come back full circle. 'I put you all here. Gave you breath. Took care of all your needs, and all this stuff, and you all are fighting about the color of your skin, or whatever, so if you don't want to do it. Let me do it.'

Gloria is optimistic for the future because she knows there's a higher power. She thinks if we, on our own, can't get it together, that higher power may be starting to. She sees a future full of little interracial kids, who know their black side and their white side, and it will all come together.

"I don't know when," she says, "but that's my prediction."

***

"How do I feel about what's happening?" Miriam says of the current state of things in America. "What's happening is so distressing, and so frightening. It's like every single thing that we've done, that we've tried to do, is being attacked. Everything, our very existence is being attacked. That's how I feel. I feel threatened, I feel frightened, and I feel determined not to give up."

Miriam has two children and eight grandchildren. At age sixty-six, she's also a great-grandmother. To her, this isn't her fight anymore. She's fighting for her children, grandchildren, great-grandchildren and beyond; she's fighting for their future in this country.

"Let me put it this way. Nelson Mandela said good and evil are always at war with one another. Have always been at war with one another, and all good men must choose. That's the best way I can describe it."

At this point, Miriam begins to cry, overwhelmed with decades of emotion. She wipes her eyes.

"You have to decide what side you're on. If you supposedly can't decide, you're on the wrong side. You have to decide. If you're saying, 'I can't decide,' then you're on the wrong side. You have to decide."

***

"It's what you learn around the people you're around, as you're growing up," says Mike. "If I'd grown up around nothing but racists, I'm pretty sure I'd have been a racist too. Of course, I think somewhere along the way I'd have had a little problem with it."

Mike thinks back to when black people started to take a stand, when Martin Luther King made his point without any violence, which pushed the buttons of people like his own stepfather.

"It's a sick country, but it's got to get better. We just need to find that cure for common stupidity. They say there's no cure for the common cold, but there is a cure for common stupidity. It's called education."

One thing that Mike has always taken pride in is that he takes a personal inventory, and tries to make himself a better person.

To this day, he knows that sometimes those old attitudes will still crop up, and he has to suppress that. If he doesn't, it would just come out as anger and craziness, which he doesn't think has much of a place in this country.

"We've got too much of it now in politics alone, never mind day to day, getting by in the world."

Action Steps For Today

Before or after dinner this evening, think about the following question. Then, tonight or tomorrow around lunch time **Keep The Conversation Going** in **Chapter 7** by posting your answers, comments, and questions.

1. The future? Do you see it getting better? Do you see that something still needs to be done?

CHAPTER 7 — THE ROAD TO REDEMPTION

"One of the most powerful things that offers hope is the road to redemption, that path to fixing one's life."

—Kevin Douglas Wright

THE END

The film I Learned It From You premiered at the historic Savor Cinema in downtown Fort Lauderdale, Florida on May 19th 2019. This event was covered by radio station WLRN-FM 91.3, which interviewed Kevin and Miriam.

Here is a replay of the radio station interview by 91.3 WLRN-FM...

https://www.wlrn.org/post/coral-springs-filmmaker-explores-power-biases-i-learned-it-you

KEEP THE CONVERSATION GOING

Please feel free to use the links below to post your answers to any of the questions asked in the book. You can also use the links below to post your own questions or comments. Check the links below for up-to-date showtimes of the documentary film version of I Learned It From You.

Web Sites

https://www.amazon.com/Learned-You-Kevin-Douglas-Wright/dp/B07WK7YXTC/

http://ilearneditfromyou.com/
http://www.kevindouglaswright.com/

https://www.amazon.com/Learned-You-Kevin-Douglas-Wright/dp/B07VTHT2RD/

Facebook

https://www.facebook.com/ILearnedItFromYou/
https://www.facebook.com/KevinFilmsBooks/

Instagram

https://www.instagram.com/ilearneditfromyou/
https://www.instagram.com/kevindouglaswright/

Twitter

https://twitter.com/ILIFYdocufilm
https://twitter.com/kevinfilmsbooks

YouTube

https://www.youtube.com/channel/
UCw8WrAOl_hHQkncEa5ZS2Mw